Level 1
Early Beginner

DreamWorks

Shrek

Davi Dias Brasil
5º ano - Tarde

Popcorn ELT Readers

Meet ... Shrek

I'm Shrek. I'm an ogre.
I live in a swamp.
I'm Princess Fiona.
I live in a dark castle
with a dragon.
Princess Fiona
Shrek

Before you read ...
What do you think?
Who is good? Who is bad?

New Words

What do these new words mean? Ask your teacher or use your dictionary.

fairy tale characters

Here are some **fairy tale characters**.

beautiful

The girl is **beautiful**.

frightened

The boy is **frightened**.

castle

This is a **castle**.

king

marry

smile

Charlie always **smiles**.

ogre

This is an **ogre**.

swamp

There is a lot of water in a **swamp**.

rescue

'Come on!'

CHAPTER ONE
'This is my swamp!'

Shrek is an ogre. He lives in a swamp. Shrek is happy there. It is a nice, quiet home.

Lord Farquaad is a very small man, but he lives in a big castle. He is not very nice.

Lord Farquaad wants to marry the beautiful Princess Fiona. He wants to be a king.

Princess Fiona lives in a dark castle with a dragon. She is sad because she can't go out.

One day, Shrek finds a donkey near the swamp. The donkey likes talking … a lot!

'I want to come with you!' says Donkey.

'No!' shouts Shrek. 'My home is nice and quiet!'

Donkey does not listen. He goes with Shrek to the swamp.

That night, Shrek finds a lot of fairy tale characters in the swamp. Now the swamp is not quiet. Shrek is angry.

'Why are you here?' he shouts.

'Lord Farquaad doesn't want fairy tale characters at the castle,' says Pinocchio.

'I want to see Lord Farquaad,' says Shrek. 'This is *my* swamp!'

'I'm coming too!' says Donkey.

'No!' says Shrek.

Donkey does not listen.

CHAPTER TWO

A princess and a dragon

Shrek and Donkey go to Lord Farquaad's castle.

'I don't want the fairy tale characters in my swamp!' says Shrek.

'Do something for me,' says Lord Farquaad. 'Rescue Princess Fiona from the dragon. Then it's your swamp.'

'OK,' says Shrek.

Shrek and Donkey walk and walk. Donkey talks ... and talks!

'Be quiet!' shouts Shrek. But he likes his new friend.

Then they see the castle.

'Come on!' says Shrek.

Shrek runs in front of Donkey. He goes to rescue Princess Fiona.

Donkey is frightened. It is dark in the castle. Suddenly Donkey is looking in the dragon's eye!

Donkey stops and talks to Dragon.

'I like your eyes,' he says. 'They are beautiful.'

Dragon is happy. Now she likes Donkey!

Shrek sees Princess Fiona in a small room. She is very beautiful.

Shrek and Princess Fiona run away from Dragon. Donkey comes too.

'Who are you?' Princess Fiona asks Shrek. 'Do you want to marry me?'

'No! I'm an ogre,' he says. 'Lord Farquaad wants to marry you.'

Then they start the long walk to Lord Farquaad's castle.

Shrek and Princess Fiona talk and talk. They play games. They have dinner.

'Come and see me in my swamp,' says Shrek.

'Thank you,' smiles Princess Fiona.

One night, Donkey is frightened. He sees Princess Fiona and she is not beautiful. At night, she is an ogre!

'Talk to Shrek,' Donkey says to her.

'I can't!' says Princess Fiona.

CHAPTER THREE
'Marry me!'

In the morning, Lord Farquaad comes with his men.

'Marry me!' he says to Princess Fiona. Lord Farquaad likes her, but Princess Fiona does not like him. She goes to his castle. Shrek is very sad.

'Princess Fiona likes you, Shrek!' says Donkey. 'She doesn't want to marry Lord Farquaad.'

Suddenly they see Dragon. Shrek and Donkey go with Dragon to Lord Farquaad's castle.

Princess Fiona is sad.

Then Shrek comes in. 'Stop!' he says. 'Fiona, I love you!'

'Shrek!' Princess Fiona is happy now.

The sun goes down. It is dark. Princess Fiona is an ogre again.

'You're beautiful!' says Shrek.

Lord Farquaad is very angry.

Suddenly Dragon comes into the castle. She eats Lord Farquaad!

Shrek and Princess Fiona marry in Shrek's swamp. They are very happy!

Real World

SWAMPS

Shrek lives in a swamp.

What is a swamp?

There is a lot of water and mud in a swamp. Many animals, birds and insects live there.

frogs

You can find frogs in swamps.

trees

alligators

This swamp has some young alligators in it. How many alligators are there?

Venus flytraps

This plant is always hungry. It eats insects!

Did you know ...?

- There are many swamps in Florida, in the USA.
- Alligators run very fast.

mosquitoes

Look at the mosquito. How many legs does it have?

snakes

Snakes like swamps! How many colours can you see on the snake?

birds

A lot of birds live in swamps. Herons eat small fish from the swamp.

What do these words mean? Find out.

mud bird insect
plant fish USA

After you read

1 True (✓) or False (✗)? Write in the box.

a) Shrek likes his swamp because it is quiet. ☑

b) Lord Farquaad lives in a small castle. ☐

c) Shrek likes Donkey. ☐

d) Donkey is always talking. ☐

e) In the day, Princess Fiona is an ogre. ☐

f) Princess Fiona marries Shrek. ☐

2 Match the questions and answers.

a) Who does Princess Fiona want to marry?

b) Who does Lord Farquaad want to marry?

c) Where does Princess Fiona live?

d) Who does Dragon eat?

e) Where does Shrek live?

i) Lord Farquaad

ii) Shrek

iii) Princess Fiona

iv) in a swamp

v) in a castle

Where's the popcorn?

Look in your book.

Can you find it?

Puzzle time!

1 Find the names and words.

a) 

b) 

c) 

D C L T O S
O A W D S R
N S H R E K
K T M A B I
E L A G I N
Y E R O O G
L T R N J N
L R Y S Y F

d) 

e) 

f) 

2a Draw lines.

b Can you walk like Shrek and his friends? Try it!

3 Circle the right word.

a) Shrek is **happy** / **angry** / **frightened** in his swamp.

b) Shrek sees the fairy tale characters. Shrek is **happy** / **angry** / **frightened**.

c) Donkey sees Dragon. He is **happy** / **angry** / **frightened**.

d) Shrek and Princess Fiona marry. They are **happy** / **angry** / **frightened**.

4 Who does Shrek meet first in the story? Put the characters in order.

Imagine ...

1 Work in groups.
Choose a character from *Shrek*.

2 Your teacher is going to read *Shrek*.
Listen and mime your character.

Chant

1 Listen and read.

Shrek's chant

2 Clap with the chant.

Shrek,	ogre,	Donkey,	Dragon
(clap)	*(clap clap)*	*(clap clap)*	*(clap clap)*

3 Say the chant.